40 DAYS: TREASURES OF DARKNESS

Alistair Matheson

"I will give you the treasures of darkness and hidden wealth of secret places, so that you may know that it is I, the Lord, the God of Israel, who calls you by your name."

ISAIAH 45:3

CONTENTS

ENDORSEMENTS

Solomon wrote: "Walk with the wise and become wise ..." (Proverbs 13:20). When you read a book you are, in effect, spending time with the author. My friend Alistair Matheson, in my opinion, is someone you'd want to spend 40 days with. A true pioneer, a credible leader and most importantly a man who knows God. Each day I know you'll be enriched by his keen insights and authentic faith.

Peter Anderson
Lead Pastor, Destiny Church Edinburgh

Alistair Matheson has a deep understanding of the revelation of the ways of God and a wonderful ability to communicate them meaningfully. These Treasures of Darkness *shine brightly, leading us into the discovery, appreciation and apprehension of the startling works of God in the most unlikely places and people. This is a devotional that will truly enrich your life.*

Steven Anderson
Apostolic Leader, Glasgow City Church

Even the night is like daytime to God. The darkest background can become a setting for the brightest of heaven's jewels. Thank you, Alistair, for sharing this treasure trove, reminding us that the light shines in the darkness and the darkness has not overcome it.

James Faddes
Pastor, Bishopbriggs Community Church

Like me, you will find a jewel on every page in this little book of treasures. Your faith will prosper and your life will be enriched.

Alex M Gillies
Senior Pastor, Victory Christian Centre, Glasgow

The God who, at Creation, separated light and darkness, calling the former day and the latter night described all he made as good. The wonders observed in daylight are just as real in darkness, though less visible. There are treasures, however - like those of our galaxy - that are best observed in darkness. Indeed, there are some treasures that are only accessible because of darkness.

Alistair Matheson, in 40 Days: Treasures of Darkness, writes of the darkness of human experience, ranging from Israel of times past to his own journey earlier in life. Yet, as happened at Creation and again at redemption, the light of grace shines in the darkness and brings forth treasures that would not otherwise be found.

Alistair follows a simple pattern through 40 days of discovery: a Bible truth, a brief narrative with insights elegantly expressed and a prayer.

40 Days: Treasures of Darkness *is much more than a daily devotional. It is a map to hidden treasure embedded in, and revealed through, times of darkness.*

I commend it to you in the belief that it will help you, not just for forty days, but through life itself.

Timothy W Jack
National Leader (2016-20), Apostolic Church UK

In a rapidly changing world, 40 Days: Treasures of Darkness *is a solid and inspirational collection of sound biblical truth, heart-warming personal stories and inspirational teaching. Each day will lead you to a deeper understanding of God's heart for humanity collectively and His incredible plan for each one of us individually. Pastor Alistair has brought together his years of experience and knowledge as 'an apostle and a friend' and distilled some of that into these beautiful devotionals. I highly recommend you taste and see!*

Ivan Parker
National Leader, Apostolic Church UK

Revelation is essential to our spiritual growth. What we see and how we see determine the way we live our lives. 40 Days: Treasures of Darkness *offer the reader an opportunity to grow in the knowledge of God and his ways. Nothing changes the human heart like seeing God. Thank you, Alistair, for this small treasure chest.*

Steve Uppal
Senior Leader, All Nations Christian Centre,
Wolverhampton

ACKNOWLEDGE-MENTS

Firstly, a big 'Thank you!' to my wife, Barbara, and son, Kenneth, who put up with me for what, as of today, has been exactly three months of lockdown. You suffered me as I pecked away for hours on end at my keyboard inside a semi-permeable membrane that welcomed all your offers of help, but failed to register too many of your requests in return! Today, you come first.

Thank you, Andy Adam, for your detailed editorial support and tutilage on what has been a first-of-its-kind for me. Andy is a *proper* writer - a former *Times* journalist and an excellent author. He never once hinted at what he really ought to have said: 'Alistair, just let me do it!' He has not requested the favour, but I highly recommend his biography, *Thomas Cochrane and the Dragon Throne*, a must-read for any-one who hasn't heard the story of Andy's step-grand-father, one of Scotland's most unsung missionary heroes.

I am humbled by the time Alan Ross took to read

and provide such positive, detailed feedback on the first half of my manuscript. Alan is a gifted prophet in the body of Christ, but his academic prowess is as impressive as his spiritual insight and his encouragement gave me the fresh impetus needed as I started to ask, *"Would thirty days maybe be better, Lord?"* Alan is one of those new friends who feels more like a long lost one and there was no way I could take the foot off the gas after his kind words.

I am so grateful also for the proof reading of Jane James, who freely provided her impressive editorial skills and experience, correcting my textual flaws and general inconsistencies. Her encouragement from early on has been more of a bolster than she appreciates. Anything lacking now is down to me.

I am also quite blown away by the generosity of my endorsers - they cannot mean me, surely? Each one is a leader I admire and love to boast about being pals with. Their approval would have sufficed, but their praise might make it difficult for my wife and son to survive the remainder of lockdown with me!

Thank you, John Caldwell, for your tips on negotiating Amazon Kindle and Print ... as your own titles roll off a seemingly continuous press. Thank you, also, for your recommendation of our excellent cover designer, Mary Findley.

I cannot neglect to thank Larry Donaldson and all my friends in Glasgow City Church who have cheerled my audio files along the way as I gingerly tested the waters - you, above all, have finally put an end to years of procrastination in attempting something like this.

And last, but certainly not least, I am indebted to those who volunteered their testimonies and contributions. To my friend John Gibson, especially, thank you for providing such living proof that the premise of this book stands up to the most rigorous test I could find. For me, Day 39 alone vindicates the project. You and Isobel are a treasure on earth for the days ahead.

FOREWORD

In writing *40 Days: Treasures of Darkness* Alistair Matheson has given Christian believers exactly the kind of resource they need for a time like this. Corona virus is reshaping every aspect of our lives. Britain's health, social, employment and educational systems are in the melting pot, not to mention its economy. Society is torn by sacrifice and devotion on one side and bitterness and recrimination on the other. One wonders where it will all end. Which side will win: the white wolf or the black wolf?

Throughout the ages Christians have found that when storms rage and the sands shift, there is only one rock to which they can cling. It is the eternal and unchanging love of God for His creation. Alistair uses Isaiah's haunting theme of 'the treasures of darkness,' to anchor his readers to that Rock and to comfort and inspire them.

He draws on biblical examples to make his case, and reinforces them with wonderful testimonies drawn from years spent as a pastor in his native Isle of Skye and in Glasgow. He shows how God creates the brightest dawn out of the blackest night; how He works better and faster in the darkness when our protests cease and we hear his voice; and how He uses our trials to make us better Christians and a comfort to those around us. He wants us to *"shine like stars in the universe, as we hold out the word of life to others."*

Nobody knows how long the global pandemic will last, nor whether others will follow in its wake. We may find that future historians divide the 21st century into B.C. (before Covid) and C.C. (continuing Covid). Indeed, towards the end of these devotional studies, Alistair considers the pandemic as a foretaste of End Times. *"The greatest display of God's glory,"* he reminds us, *"will emerge from the deepest shades of darkness."*

I started by saying that these studies were written for an extraordinary time, but their value is timeless. This little book should not be permitted to go out of print.

Andrew Adam
West Monkton,
Somerset,
June 2020

INTRODUCTION

40 Days: Treasures of Darkness was written entirely during the Corona virus pandemic of 2020 and is built upon the biblical premise that all good things begin in the dark.

Darkness covered the face of the deep before God first said, *"Let there be light!"* The order of dark-then-light is quickly repeated six times as we read of evening coming before - not after - morning, on each day of creation.

The beginning of Jesus' earthly ministry is described by Matthew as a light dawning on a people sitting in darkness.

And what of Jesus' own teaching? While believers cling to the certain hope of life after death, Jesus Himself was more inclined to stress the impossibility of life before it. Just as night before day, so death before life is the order.

The Apostle Paul went on to teach that it was only

because he had been crucified with Christ, that he was now able to truly live on earth.

Again and again, the redemption story is one of darkness followed by light, night then day, death then life.

Ultimately, the Book of Revelation completes the narrative with the promise of no more night as the Day to come will be endless, lit up for all by the radiance of Christ Himself.

The theme of *40 Days: Treasures of Darkness* is not a morbid preoccupation with darkness and death. It is a message of glorious hope for anyone struggling with the stuff of a broken world. God is not shut out by the night; He owns it.

In Jesus, darkness is the threshold of a new day.

If Jesus is yours, your lowest moment is not the end of the story; it offers the beginning of a hope, peace and joy that nothing in this world can either give or take away.

Alistair J Matheson
23rd June 2020

1 – TREASURES OF DARKNESS

"I will give you the treasures of darkness and hidden wealth of secret places ..."

Isaiah 45:3

Listen to these wonderful words, spoken through the prophet Isaiah, with ears of faith and a believing heart!

I say that because this passage, supernaturally inspired by the Spirit of God, has been greeted with scepticism by those who see the Bible as just another historical document.

They say these words, spoken to Cyrus the Great, couldn't possibly have been written by Isaiah, since

Cyrus lived some 140 years later! We know that his Syrian empire overpowered the Babylonians and helped the Jews to return home.

But is it not the nature of prophecy to speak into the future?

Isaiah was the self-same eagle-eyed prophet who, seven centuries before the event, foresaw the birth of Immanuel from a virgin's womb. He wrote the words of Jesus' first message in Nazareth and saw the Spirit of God anoint Him. He also described in amazing detail the atonement of Christ's death!

It was the power of the prophetic word, calling out his name more than a century before his birth, that moved Cyrus to this wonderful moment in Jewish history. The historian Josephus quoted King Cyrus as saying, "... *God Almighty ... foretold my name by the prophets ... that I should build him a house at Jerusalem ..."*

This is the same Isaiah who spoke of glorious light shining out of deep darkness in chapter 60, and of the revelation of things never before seen by the natural eye in chapter 64. In today's verse he directs Cyrus to hoards of treasure buried in Babylon. He is the same Isaiah who now invites you to discover unspeakable riches in the unlikeliest – and darkest – of places.

Prayer:

Lord, find in me this day a believing heart and expectant eyes. By Your Spirit, help me discover priceless treasures found in places I might never think to look. Show me things which my eye has not yet seen and my ear has not yet heard. Amen.

2 – PLUNDERING HELL!

"I'll lead you to buried treasures, secret caches of valuables – confirmations that it is, in fact, I, God, the God of Israel, who calls you by your name."

Isaiah 45:3, The Message

The late, great evangelist Reinhard Bonnke wrote and preached passionately about 'plundering hell to populate heaven', occupying the most hostile territories to enrich the Kingdom of God with gemstones of salvation. His point was simple and clear: like treasures stored in underground vaults, the most glorious futures are held in waiting in the darkest places.

Apparently, ancient conquerors would call upon sorcerers to lead them to the hidden riches of people plundered. They would use the plunder to pay their armies and take the conquest to regions beyond. Babylon's plunder was immense. Before Cyrus, Nebuchadnezzar had amassed great caches of wealth to be bunkered and hidden around the Euphrates River. According to the Roman writer, Pliny, when the Persians took over from the Babylonians, Cyrus plundered 34,000 pounds in weight of gold, and much more besides, from the conquest of what is Turkey today, and this became the very treasure used to fund the rebuilding of the temple in Jerusalem, written of in the Book of Ezra.

For me, it is an amazing picture of Christ rising victorious from the bunker of death, to build up His church using souls rescued from the powers of darkness. Paul told the Ephesians that the resurrected Christ, having *"captured the enemy and seized the booty,"* (Eph. 4:8, The Message), ascended in triumph far above the heavens and, from that exalted throne, poured out His gifts upon the church, establishing, equipping, energising His body through people once held captive to sin ... the treasures of darkness!

Prayer:

> Lord, help me to see darkness as an opportunity for light. Will You show me today something of what You saw for me when You cap-

tured me by Your great love. And when I look around me, at the neediest people in the darkest of situations, help me to catch a glimmer of what You might have in mind for them. Amen.

3 – SHATTERED BRONZE

"Thus says the Lord to Cyrus His anointed, ... '... I will shatter the doors of bronze and cut through their iron bars. I will give you the treasures of darkness and hidden wealth of secret places ...'"

Isaiah 45:1-3

According to the Greek historian, Herodotus, the walls of ancient Babylon were interspersed with *"a hundred massy gates of brass, whose hinges and frames were of the same metal."* The same God who watched Nebuchadnezzar stockpile the treasures of the known world in Babylon, delivered Babylon into the hand of the Syrians, ordained Cyrus ruler of

Syria ... and placed Jerusalem in the heart of Cyrus!

History is not a chaotic explosion of haphazard events in a world out of control. The rise of Cyrus the Great for the restoration of the Jews was a divine plan revealed by Isaiah more than a century before Cyrus was born. Ours is a God who *"causes all things to work together for good to those who love [Him], to those who are called according to His purpose."* (Romans 8:28)

Be wary of simplistic ideas like, *God runs the church and the devil runs the world!* Hidden treasures are not stored in such shallow thinking. God and the devil are active in both fields, but God is in ultimate control. Satan tries to darken our minds with depressive thoughts, but God, towering over His creation, exploits every twisted scheme to produce wonderful outcomes.

Pause for a moment and consider this: God is in charge of Babylon and Babylon only does what God allows and what He can use. As Solomon wrote, *"the wealth of the sinner is stored up for the righteous."* (Proverbs 13:22)

So what blessings might God be preparing in even the blackest, most menacing moments of human history?

Prayer:

   Almighty Lord, help me to see foreboding

'gates of brass' and their dark 'iron bars' as impregnable only for a season, waiting to be shattered at the moment of Your choosing, serving Your higher purpose and releasing future blessing beyond my comprehension. Amen.

4 – WISDOM

*"… If you seek [wisdom] as silver and
search for her as for hidden treasures;
then you will discern the fear of the
Lord and discover the knowledge of
God. For the Lord gives wisdom; from
His mouth come knowledge and understanding. He stores up sound wisdom
for the upright …."*

Proverbs 2:4-7a

Today, we move back in time to Israel's glory days.
Solomon here uses the same Hebrew word for 'treasures' later used in Isaiah chapter 45. The word,
interestingly, is 'matmon', thought by some to be
the root of 'mammon' (money), which Jesus ex-
posed as such a great rival to God in the hearts of

men.

Babylon's 'matmon' was hidden in the darkness of secret underground vaults. Centuries before Cyrus, King Solomon's lavish wealth was displayed openly and astonished the world. Yet Solomon had treasures which he cherished even more than his 1.4 trillion pound estate: the riches of wisdom. Before ascending to the throne, it was these greater riches that Solomon had asked God for, and thankfully God did not disappoint.

Even Solomon had difficult moments in life. On one occasion two rival mothers came to him. The baby of one of them had died and each woman claimed that the surviving child was hers. What was he to do? He demonstrated how, even in the absence of hard facts and reliable knowledge, wisdom will still save the day.

A pearl of wisdom shone in the darkness of the women's conflict. *"Cut the baby in half,"* Solomon ordered: *"In this way each of you can have part of him."* Of course, the true mother could never let this happen, and it was her to whom Solomon had the infant restored.

Jesus displayed similar flashes of inspiration in situations where He seemed cornered by Pharisees hellbent on destroying His ministry. Rhetorical questions flashed like swords from his mouth, which His confounded opponents simply could not answer.

Wasn't this wonderful resource, the wisdom of Heaven, promised to us too? Jesus told us what to expect when we face intimidating odds. *"The Holy Spirit will teach you in that very hour what you ought to say."* (Luke 12:12)

Are you struggling in the dark? Maybe you need the treasure of God's wisdom now?

Prayer:

> Lord, thank You for the prayer James told us to pray, a prayer we are to ask with absolute certainty of Your provision: *"... If any of you lacks wisdom, let him ask of God, who gives to all generously and without reproach, and it will be given to him ..."* (James 1:5ff) Lord, reveal to me the treasures of Your wisdom today. Amen.

5 – FROWNING PROVIDENCE

"He reveals mysteries from the darkness and brings the deep darkness into light."

Job 12:22

The 18th century hymn-writer, William Cowper, wrote of the mysteries of darkness in a poem entitled, *'God Moves in a Mysterious Way'*:

> *Deep in unsearchable mines of never failing skill,*
> *He treasures up His bright designs and works His sovereign will.*
> *Ye fearful saints, fresh courage take: the clouds you so much dread*
> *Are big with mercy and shall break in blessings on your head.*

The poem has a personal significance for me. My family home for centuries past has been the Isle of Skye where I returned to work as a pastor and schoolteacher for twenty years. In the 1920s my grandfather Kenneth emigrated from Glendale to the USA. For five years he worked for the Ford Motor Company, saving up for his wife and three children to join him. The youngest child was my dad, who was fourteen.

Then disaster struck. My grandmother ran a grocery store and she was fumbling her way home in the dark when her oil lamp slipped from her hand, exploded and set fire to her frock. She was rushed to hospital but six days later her husband in Detroit received a six-word telegram: "Effie dead. Lamp explosion. Children well." The American dream was over.

Back home in Glendale an elder had to break the news to the children. He entered their cottage at a complete loss what to say. Then he saw a framed text on the mantelpiece and thanked God before reading Cowper's words to them:

> *Judge not the Lord by feeble sense, but trust Him for His grace;*
> *Behind a frowning providence He hides a smiling face.*

I never knew my grandfather, but I knew and loved my father for forty-four very special years. He was a wonderful man, fifty years my senior. I can still hear his rich voice and my heart warms as I visualise his smiling face. But for the frown of that dark winter night on the Isle of Skye he would have grown up an American, married a different girl and had different children. And I would never have known his smile.

America never had my dad to lose him. But that dark night delivered to me, my children and my grandchildren a treasure beyond price.

Prayer:

> Unsearchable God, I thank You that You are also my loving and all-knowing Heavenly Father, the One who knows the end from the beginning, able to make the darkest clouds burst with blessings on our heads. Come into our darkness today and cause Your hope to shine. Amen.

6 – MYSTERIES OF DARKNESS

"He makes the nations great, then destroys them; He enlarges the nations, then leads them away. He deprives of intelligence the chiefs of the earth's people and makes them wander in a pathless waste. They grope in darkness with no light ..."

Job 12:23-25

Although some have suggested that Job was the first book in the Bible to be written, scholars are uncertain when the author lived. Others think the book may have been produced in the days of Nebuchadnezzar and the rise and fall of ancient Babylon. Nebuchadnezzar's derangement (Daniel 4:31-33) would fit well with God bringing great nations low and causing their rulers to wander in pathless wastes.

But while Job speaks of God bringing mysteries to light, he doesn't say that we need to be in the dark. God has never concealed His will from those ready to see and hear.

Didn't the prophet Amos (3:7) say, *"Surely the Lord God does nothing unless He reveals His secret counsel to His servants the prophets"*? Similarly, didn't the prophet Jeremiah declare that Nebuchadnezzar would be raised up to judge the backslidden Jews, and that, after Babylon had served its purpose, His judgement would turn on Babylon too? And didn't the prophet Isaiah (45:1-3) prophesy well in advance that King Cyrus would plunder Babylon's *"treasures of darkness"*?

God could not have spelled out His plans more clearly but until they unfolded they remained as much a mystery as Babylon's underground bunkers! God was at work behind the menace of Babylon's rise and the devastation of its fall. His prophets painted a very clear picture. He wasn't concealing His purposes in riddles and enigmas and He does not do so today.

Christ has created His church to be today's prophet of light in a dark world – a people of the day, before the day breaks. Listen to how the apostle Paul lays upon us, as Christ's embodiment, the mantle of the prophet: *"... 'Things which eye has not seen and ear has not heard, and which have not entered the heart of man, all that God has prepared for those who love Him,'* **for to us God revealed them through the Spirit**; *for the Spirit searches all things, even the depths of God."* (I Corinthians 2:9-10; emphasis mine)

Prayer:

> Lord, thank you for birthing me in the light, as a child of the day. Thank You for giving me Your Holy Spirit Who Jesus said would take Your word, and speak to me, and disclose to me what is to come! Speak to me again today. Amen.

7 – JANICE

*"To appoint unto them that mourn
in Zion, to give unto them beauty for
ashes, the oil of joy for mourning,
the garment of praise for the spirit of
heaviness; that they might be called
trees of righteousness, the planting of
the Lord, that he might be glorified."*

Isaiah 61:3, KJV

I know an amazing woman called Janice McBride. Hers is an incredible story, both awful and wonderful, of deep darkness and glorious light.

A wartime child in the Clydebank blitz, Janice recalls the sight of mutilated bodies on the streets. But the carnage of her home life was no kinder. Surrounded by alcoholism, she never knew her father and was horrendously abused by her mother and a string of her live-in boyfriends. Mum knew what these men were doing to Janice and did nothing to defend her. She frequently told Janice how she'd rejected an offer of adoption by a nurse when she was born: *"It wasn't because I loved you, Janice, because I don't. You are my sin."*

After growing up, Janice married an American serviceman and moved to the States. It was here, as her own predictably miserable marriage was about to fail, that Janice heard the Gospel. For the first time, light began to break into her life as she received Jesus Christ as her personal Saviour.

If anyone could wish history re-written, it's Janice. Just to wipe it all out and start again. Not in luxury, just pain free, maybe in the home of a kind nurse longing for a child of her own?

Janice's response to her long childhood nightmare might startle some people, but not those who know Jesus Christ and understand the Bible narrative of bright light shining out of deep darkness.

"Today," Janice once told me, *"I reach into the lives of people in the trauma of war zones and I have more than words to bring into their brokenness. Today, I can speak hope into the lives of victims of unspeakable abuse and the casualties of broken families – I tell them that forgiveness will deliver them from the imprisonment of their past, and when they tell me, 'You don't know what I've been through, Janice," I reply, 'No, I've been through*

worse.'

"I wouldn't change my past," Janice said, *"It's given me a ministry."*

Prayer:

> Lord, I thank You that when You enter in, pains too dark to bear can produce glories too bright to contain. Touch the untouchable moments of my past and cause Your light to begin to shine. Bring out in me the treasures of darkness. Amen.

8 – NIGHT THEN DAY

"In the beginning God created the heaven and the earth. And the earth was without form, and void; and darkness was upon the face of the deep. And the Spirit of God moved upon the face of the waters. And God said, 'Let there be light': and there was light. And God saw the light, that it was good: and God divided the light from the darkness. And God called the light Day, and the darkness he called Night. And the evening and the morning were the first day."

Genesis 1:1-5, KJV

Today, let's travel back to the dawn of time. Have you ever considered that the sequence of God's Creation was darkness followed by light? Perfect black covered 'the face of the deep' before the first sunburst. Everything God has ever done in the entire cosmos began out of deep darkness.

In our smallness, we so easily confine everything to the tiny frame of our limited vision. When we say things like, *'As surely as night follows day ...,'* we betray the assumption that everything begins with our ability to see it, rather than what was there before we awoke.

"... And the evening and the morning were the first day." Night then day: that's God's order. The Jewish people still understand this when they begin their Sabbath at sunset on Friday, but most of us have lost the fundamental creation principle of darkness *then* light.

This is not 'splitting hairs', just an offer of definite, wonderful hope to anyone in the depths of a dark night. Friend, where there is no night, there will be no dawn. This is more than a creation principle; it is the pattern of salvation revealed through the arrival of Jesus Christ.

Listen to how our Saviour enters the world: *"... The people who were sitting in the darkness saw a great Light, and those who were sitting in the land of the shadow of death, upon them a Light dawned."* (Matthew 4:16)

Are you are sitting in spiritual, or psychological, darkness today? No matter how heavy its weight, the moment you invite Jesus in, He becomes your dawn, your new day, the Light that pierces through fear, anxiety, confusion and the things of the night.

Prayer:

Lord Jesus, if You are the Light of the world, then You can surely brighten my heart and illuminate my mind. Guide me by Your Holy Spirit today into the light of Your wonderful Word. Amen.

9 – BABYLON

"God's message to his anointed, to Cyrus, whom he took by the hand to give the task of taming the nations, of terrifying their kings – He gave him free rein, no restrictions: 'I'll go ahead of you, clearing and paving the road. I'll break down bronze city gates, smash padlocks, kick down barred entrances. I'll lead you to buried treasures, secret caches of valuables – confirmations that it is, in fact, I, God, the God of Israel, who calls you by your name."

Isaiah 45:1–3, The Message

I return again to the theme text for this devotional series because there is so much to unlock from ancient Babylon.

Beyond its gates of bronze and bunkers of gold, Babylon's Hanging Gardens were one of the Seven Wonders of the ancient world, another showpiece of an empire in its pomp. Babylon was held in awe as the great dominion of the day ... until the rise of the Syrian empire of King Cyrus.

Babylon had been a source of trepidation to the Jews, casting an overwhelming spectre of gloom over their national morale – and rightly so, when God Himself had declared them to be His instrument of judgement against a backslidden people.

But now Judah's captivity was over; its judgement was complete and Babylon had served its purpose. To allow the return of the Jewish exiles and to fund the refurbishment of the temple, the same God who had enlisted the powers of Nebuchadnezzar for judgement now raised up the mighty Cyrus for restoration.

The prophet who foretold these events was the same Isaiah who later announced, *"'For My thoughts are not your thoughts, nor are your ways My ways,' declares the Lord. 'For as the heavens are higher than the earth, so are My ways higher than your ways and My thoughts than your thoughts.'"* (Isaiah 55:8-9)

Consider just some of God's unfathomable ways. In Babylon God overcomes our darkness. His timing is perfect and causes impregnable walls to crumble.

He turns the punishment of the past into a source of blessing. He halts unbridled cruelty and uses its spoils to resource His restoration programme.

Prayer:

> Lord, I marvel that what the devil has intended for evil, You are able to so quickly turn to the good. Almighty God, Redeemer, Deliverer and Restorer, shine out of the darkness that surrounds and reveal Your wonderful promise of a new day. Amen.

10 – A FUTURE AND A HOPE

"'For I know the plans that I have for you,' declares the Lord, 'plans for welfare and not for calamity to give you a future and a hope.'"

Jeremiah 29:11

A maxim of the sociologist Alvin Gouldner is that *"context is everything."* It is of utmost importance for our understanding the Bible. Few texts have been so often removed from their place of meaning as Jeremiah 29:11. In order to understand what Jeremiah was saying, we need to appreciate to whom he was speaking and why.

He spoke these words early in the Babylonian exile, a judgment of God upon His people which lasted 70 years. They had hardened their hearts and rejected His prophets. The judgment turned out to be God's therapy; it brought them to their senses and turned them back to Him.

The people were not like some conscientious teenager desperate to do well and afraid of letting parents down. A more accurate picture would be of a spoiled child begging for a curfew to be lifted, and a father holding his ground: *'No! You're grounded for as long as it takes until you change your attitude and learn respect. One day you'll thank me for it!'*

This is how The Message renders Jeremiah 29:10-11: *"This is God's Word on the subject: 'As soon as Babylon's seventy years are up and not a day before, I'll show up and take care of you as I promised and bring you back home. I know what I'm doing. I have it all planned out – plans to take care of you, not abandon you, plans to give you the future you hope for.'"*

Hope for the future requires surrender today ... and a patient willingness to see through difficult times too!

God still has a way of using seasons of affliction to turn His people's hearts back to Him. Make no mistake, God is in charge of national and global crises. So when such distresses do come, His beloved children would do well to heed the words of American psychiatrist Myron F Weiner: *"Don't waste a crisis!"*

Use the moment of darkness as a wake-up call to

seek God's face again.

A future and a hope ... for all prepared to wait: yet more treasures of darkness!

Prayer:

> Loving Heavenly Father, forgive me for my days of wandering from You, for any other gods I have allowed to take Your place in the priorities of my life. Thank You that You discipline the child You love, and that, when I fail to heed Your word, You care enough to use the consequences of my disobedience to turn my attention back to You. Amen.

11 – GOD'S BABYLON

"Arise and go down to the potter's house, and there I will announce My words to you."

Jeremiah 18:2

Perhaps the greatest hidden treasure of Babylon is the power of God to reveal redemptive purpose out of suffering and loss; to weave scenes of tragic devastation into a great master plan, for the ultimate good of those He loves.

At the beginning of the Babylonian exile, Jeremiah prophesied, *"… When seventy years are completed I will punish the king of Babylon …"* (Jeremiah 25:12), but until that long night of history was over, Babylon was to be *"the potter's house."*

God - not Nebuchadnezzar - was the potter, and Babylon was His chosen place to scrap and re-form a nation that had become a marred vessel, disfigured into something He never intended. When a grieving Jeremiah saw God's judgement coming and warned his people, he was beaten and put in stocks at the city gate.

These were unpalatable years for those unable to see light at the end of the tunnel, let alone inside it. Even one of the later psalmists groaned from the exile of the Potter's house, *"By the rivers of Babylon we sat and wept ... How can we sing the songs of the Lord while in a foreign land."* (Psalm 137:1, 4)

And yet, this place of banishment – like's Joseph's pit, Jonah's fish, Daniel's den, Paul's dungeon ... and Jesus' tomb – would be looked back to, from the other side of dawn, as the source of an explosion of glorious light.

Have you ever felt immobilised, confined, even scared, by events far beyond your power to understand, much less survive? That's just what Babylon was to the Jews. But it was God's Babylon, the House of the Potter.

Prayer:

> Lord, let me take Your hand today and be led in the light of Your Word. Help me not to kick, scream and struggle against the circumstances

of a fallen world that I cannot change. Grant me Your grace to embrace Your greater purpose as sovereign over all things. Remove from and work into my life whatever You will, that I might fully be molded into the vessel you intend me to be. Amen.

12 – BABYLON'S BRIGHTEST

"As for these four youths, God gave them knowledge and intelligence in every branch of literature and wisdom; Daniel even understood all kinds of visions and dreams."

Daniel 1:17

Towards the end of the Book of Daniel, an angel appears to Daniel and says, *"Those who have insight will shine brightly like the brightness of the expanse of heaven, and those who lead the many to righteousness, like the stars forever and ever."* (12:3). Clearly the angel was speaking of the likes of Daniel and his friends.

Before we consider these stars, we must think about

the setting God chose for them in which to shine. Babylon traces its origins to the condemned Tower of Babel of Genesis chapter 11 and has its final great tumble in Revelation chapter 18. It stands for all that is most wicked in a world system that has raised itself up against God Himself.

For the apostle John, Babylon was a pseudonym for Rome, where the church would endure centuries of persecution, where *"all the nations have drunk of the wine of the passion of her immorality, and the kings of the earth have committed acts of immorality with her, and the merchants of the earth have become rich by the wealth of her sensuality."* (Revelation 12:3)

The brutish Babylonian empire, where a generation of exiled Jews found it impossible to *'sing the Lord's song,'* was the very place where Daniel, Shadrach, Meshach and Abednego shone like stars in the heavens, where they rose to the highest of public offices, and did so without compromising their faith, 'without eating the king's meat.'

Few would deny the wickedness of the world and some people never get past lamenting it! Others see the darkness as the reason they are here; they get right in amongst it and, what's more, they even discover they aren't the only lights. They get together with other light-bearers to turn their flicker to a flame; they see God above their earthly rulers and He clears a way for them to shine as treasures of darkness!

Prayer:

Dear Lord, help me see that it is the darkest places that most need Your light. Keep me pure, by Your Spirit and Your word, never compromising the integrity of my walk with You. Send out Your people today as Your salt and Your light. Amen.

13 – PRAYER

"In the early morning, while it was still dark, Jesus got up, left the house and went away to a secluded place, and was praying there."

Mark 1:35

Jesus had been up late the night before, casting out demons and healing many who were sick. These days must have been all-consuming as He poured Himself into the needs of the multitudes. After such times, it wasn't unusual for Jesus to retreat to His Father, sometimes in remote places during the night hours.

The psalmist (127:1-2) had taught that it's pointless to labour hard into the night … *if* God's not in charge. But Jesus journeyed into the night to *meet* with God. And it was often in this unseen place that His work began.

In John's gospel, Jesus repeatedly talks of doing nothing from His own initiative, of saying only what He heard the Father say and doing only what He saw the Father do.

In Luke's gospel, we read that it was after a night of prayer that He came down the mountain to call His disciples? And was it not from the lonely darkness of Gethsemane that He stirred His sleeping disciples saying, "*Get up, it's time to go ...*", before stepping out to launch the salvation act of mankind.

The greatest treasures of history have been sourced in the dark. The night-time of human need is where God enters, never where He leaves. As a pastor, I have always found funeral services to be the most spiritually fertile soil for gospel seed to take root. These are places of keenly felt need, occasions when mourners meet the Comforter and the poor in spirit sometimes stumble their way into a Hope that will never disappoint.

The wonderful *works* of God are displayed in their glory in the light of day, but the wonders of His *ways* are often discovered in a lonely, dark place, where there is nowhere to turn.

"*Darkness and light are alike to [Him]*" (Psalm 139:12) and He can speak to us any time. But sometimes He gets through better when nothing else can help ... and no one else is there.

Prayer:

Lord, I thank You that in the place of felt need, even tiredness, I can come to You knowing that Your truth and Your ways are to be found in Your precious presence. By Your Spirit, fill me with the awareness that You are with me now. Speak to me through Your word, I ask, and lead me in the way I should go. In Jesus' name, I ask. Amen.

14 – BETHEL

*"Surely the Lord is in this place, and I
did not know it."*

Genesis 28:16

A plotter and a deceiver, Jacob was fleeing for his life
from the brother whose birthright he had stolen,
heading for Haran on the wrong side of the Euphrates, the very place God had told his grandfather to
move on from. Tired and stressed, the sun now set,
Jacob found a stone for a pillow and lay down to
sleep on the darkest night of his young life.

It was also the night of his spiritual awakening,
the moment he saw angels ascending and descending back and forth between Heaven and him. It
was the night when his father's God became his God
too, when he personally received Abraham's promise of a multitude of descendants, and when God

even got Him thinking about you and me: *"... in your descendants shall all the families of the earth be blessed."* (Genesis 28:14)

In the unlikeliest of times, places and circumstances, Jacob had stumbled into *"the gate of heaven."* (Genesis 28:17) Who would have thought that this could be where a sinner running from the land of promise would meet God? Certainly not Jacob! *"Surely God is in this place,"* he said, *"and I did not know it."* From now on, that place would bear a new name: Bethel, the house of God.

Why should we be surprised? This is the same God who spent the night in the stable when the hotel was full; who stayed over with Zacchaeus when there were religious homes a-plenty to choose from; who enters the lives of the sick rather than while away the hours with those in no need of the Physician.

And why do we despair when days are dark, hearts are troubled, minds are distressed, livelihoods are under threat, when the strong falter and the wise come short?

These are exactly the places where God is most likely to show up!

Prayer:

Lord, I see again that it's the moment of weakness, need and darkness that you delight to enter. When I'm strong, I rely on me; but when I'm weak, I have only You. '*Only*' You? O Lord, turn that into '*You only!*' Speak to my heart through Your word and fill my mind with your thoughts today! Amen.

15 – BORN AGAIN

"… He took our sin-dead lives and
made us alive in Christ."

Ephesians 2:5, The Message

It was 2am on Saturday 6th February 1982 and bitterly cold. I was shivering in the darkness outside my hall of residence in Glasgow University. I had lost my keys and could barely remember where I'd spent the hours partying. One window was lit up against the blackness of the night and I launched a handful of pebbles at it.

Paul came to the window. We knew each other. The last time we'd been out, his friend had supplied me with marijuana that I mixed with far too much alcohol, leaving me flat on my back in an outside stairwell in the city, physically unable to move or even call for help.

My life was a mess. My overdraft limit was reached. I barely attended classes and was close to eviction from my residence. A chain-smoking nervous wreck, my ever expanding week-end binges had now squeezed out the weeks in between. Even my more riotous friends were now withdrawing as my personality changed. It was serious, and everyone knew it.

I have no idea how it happened but Paul and I began to talk about God. As I began to tell him about an Indian cult leader who had converted a friend of mine, Paul reached for a book on his shelf and said, "Listen to what The Bible says."

As he read, a heavy weight fell upon me. God's presence filled the room. I knew I was living in complete rejection of Him. Tears spilled from my eyes as I whispered, over and over, "Forgive me, Jesus ... Forgive me, Jesus ..." Paul looked up, startled, and asked, "What's happening, Alistair?" In a moment, he too was weeping his way back to God.

Around twelve Christians lived in that large residence, and none of them had any idea of what God was doing under their roof at four o'clock that winter morning, when a pre-dawn sunburst lit up a blackened life. By the end of the following year the band of twelve grew to thirty-five. And it all began with the most hopeless wreck of a soul that God could find.

Prayer:

Lord, I thank You that there is no heart too hard for You to break into; no life so dysfunctional that You cannot turn it around; no sinner so darkened that you cannot make him or her a light bearer. Use me as Your instrument today, Lord, to continue seeking and saving that which is lost. **Amen.**

16 – SAUL

"… Attaining to all the wealth that comes from the full assurance of understanding, resulting in a true knowledge of God's mystery, that is, Christ Himself, in whom are hidden all the treasures of wisdom and knowledge."

Colossians 2:2–3

The more I read the New Testament, the more I marvel at the revelation which flows from the pen of the apostle Paul. How did he come up with such wisdom about doctrines like righteousness by faith, new creations in Christ and our adoption as the children of God?

'Ah,' says the scholar, 'they all originate in the Old Testament.'

That may be so, but without Paul they would never

have become crystal clear, nor would they have had such impact on the Christian faith. No other writer ignited spiritual dynamite as Paul did! How did he produce these history-changing teachings?

Paul's epistles were not penned in the ivory tower of academia. His experience of a rabbinical school had turned him into an intensely religious, zealous and angry man. As a Pharisee he was all heat and no light, hell-bent on destroying the followers of Jesus Christ.

What turned Saul (as he was originally known) from using his knowledge to tie people up with the chains of dead religion, into the Paul who set hearers gloriously free with the gospel of Jesus? It happened on the road to Damascus; he was brought to his knees and physically blinded in an encounter with Jesus Christ.

Humbled and pathetic, he was led by the hand into the city. For three days he was isolated and helpless until God used a man called Ananias to restore his sight and minister the Holy Spirit to him. It was the Holy Spirit who unlocked the vaults of understanding in Paul's mind.

Ananias gave him this message: *"I am sending you to open [Gentile] eyes so that they may turn from darkness to light."* (Acts 26:17-18) Paul's missionary journeys and his ministry to the Gentiles extended deep into Europe. They ensured that the light that had broken into his darkness would one day become yours and mine too.

Prayer:

> Dear Lord, how I thank You that I do not need to climb a mountain to see the light! I thank You that Your light so often begins to shine in places of darkness, weakness and confinement. Thank You for the day Your light first shone into my life. Enter my weakness and display Your power today, I ask, in Jesus' name. Amen.

17 – GOD'S JAIL-BIRDS

"When they had struck them with many blows, they threw them into prison, commanding the jailer to guard them securely; and he, having received such a command, threw them into the inner prison and fastened their feet in the stocks. But about midnight Paul and Silas were praising and singing hymns to God ..."

Acts 16: 23-25

Come and join me on a prison visit! Not to any old prison, but the one in Philippi from which Paul and

Silas were in no hurry to escape! The story in Acts 16 is among the most heart-lifting scenes in all of the Acts of the Apostles! But first, let's go back a bit.

Paul and Silas had been trying to spread the Gospel in western Asia when the Holy Spirit stopped them in their tracks. God, who often launches us on our most important journeys by closing a door, explained things to Paul in a dream. He was being sent to Europe to make his first converts and plant his first church there.

Paul arrived in the Greek city of Philippi and, after leading Lydia to Christ, cast out an evil spirit from a fortune telling slave girl. This was a blessing to her but did not help her owner's income. The incident threw the city into confusion and landed Paul and Silas in stocks in the deepest recesses of a jail.

I light-heartedly think of Paul as a 'jail-bird preacher', not just because he was forever in and out of prison, but because he knew how to sing while inside! Contrast the weeping Psalmist who groaned about being unable to sing the Lord's song in captivity (Psalm 137) with Paul and Silas – that's where their praise and worship time began.

Words cannot describe the gratitude I have for the example Paul and Silas gave us that night, taking us to whole new heights in the lowest of depths. Remember that beautiful verse of comfort, *"Weeping may last for the night, but joy comes in the morning!"* (Psalm 30:5) Paul didn't need it! Why should they wait for the morning when joy was to be found in the night? They discovered treasures of darkness!

Prayer:

> Forgive us, Lord, for the moments we take our eyes off Jesus, the One who, *"... for the joy set before Him ... endured the cross."* (Hebrews 12:2) Lord, in the midst of my difficulties, things Paul might have called *"momentary, light afflictions,"* (II Corinthians 4:17), I stop right now. I put these things down, and I praise you with all my heart that You are here, in the midst of it all! Hallelujah!

18 – JOY!

"... And the prisoners were listening to them; and suddenly there came a great earthquake, so that the foundations of the prison house were shaken; and immediately all the doors were opened and everyone's chains were unfastened. When the jailer awoke and saw the prison doors opened, he drew his sword and was about to kill himself, supposing that the prisoners had escaped. But Paul cried out with a loud voice, saying, 'Do not harm yourself, for we are all here!' ..."

Acts 16:26-28

Paul and Silas were not minded to leave! Lobbying politicians and crowd-funding their legal fees was not on their programme! These men were now evangelists to the prison community. And why on earth would they want to be on the outside, anyway, when they were already free on the inside, and when the glory of God had so filled the prison? Easier to drag a miner away from a gold strike than to get Paul and Silas out of that jail!

This was the same Paul who would one day write to the Philippians from yet another prison: *"... I want you to know, brothers and sisters, that what has happened to me has actually served to advance the gospel. As a result, it has become clear throughout the whole palace guard and to everyone else that I am in chains for Christ."* (Philippians 1:12-13)

Among the Philippians who received that letter may have been those who *"were listening to them"* that night in Philippi, who, after being freed from their chains, chose to remain in the prison, now captives of Christ, rather than walk through open doors to so called freedom. When Paul later wrote the 'prison epistles' from Rome, he described himself as *"Christ's prisoner."* (Philemon 1:1; Ephesians 3:1) He didn't see himself as a prisoner of the city authorities or as a victim of the Romans, but as an *"ambassador in chains"* (Ephesians 6:20) whose true 'Jailer' was Jesus.

Do you know what scholars call Paul's prison epistle to the Philippians? The 'Epistle of Joy'! Joy ...

another treasure of darkness! That was the place chosen by Paul to pen the words: *"Rejoice in the Lord always. I will say it again: Rejoice!"* (Philippians 4:4)

Prayer:

> Dear Lord, when I find myself confined in the lowest moment, I thank You that You supply the grace to see You, not life's circumstances, as the One in charge! Thank You for the grace you gave Paul and Silas, the spirit that declared: *'I don't want out; I want You in!'* As I fill these moments with Your praise, Lord, will you fill them with Your glory, that all who hear me and see me might discover Your freedom too! Amen.

19 – PURE GOLD

"... That the proof of your faith, being more precious than gold which is perishable, even though tested by fire, may be found to result in praise and glory and honour at the revelation of Jesus Christ."

I Peter 1:7

One tradition has it that Peter's 'testing by fire' was an allusion to Nero's scapegoating of the church for the burning of Rome and the horrendous persecution that followed. Like his contemporary Paul, Peter apparently knew what the inside of a Roman jail cell looked like, and what a public execution felt like. Their faith was forged by trials that served only to fuel their passion for Christ.

Today's developed world enjoys levels of peace and prosperity quite unprecedented in the history of mankind. The social and economic comforts of our churches, and the tolerance and protections we benefit from, could barely be in greater contrast to the world of the people to whom the New Testament letters were originally written.

For them, the return of Christ and the promise of future glories were far more attractive than we can appreciate. The believer's future hope was grasped, clung to, preached of and sung about with fervour. The supernatural, comforting presence of the Holy Spirit in the midst of such fiery affliction was so much more precious than most of us realise.

Until ...

Until our earthly comforts and securities are threatened. Until we're awakened to our fragility by moments of bereavement or loss. Until we're unfairly treated for doing what was right. These are the moments when what is, or what is not, within us is revealed, and what is good begins to shine.

What emerged from the early church's smelter was pure gold! And what did that gold look like? Peter describes the treasure of their darkness in the very next verse: "... *Though you have not seen Him, you love Him, and though you do not see Him now, but believe in Him, you greatly rejoice with joy inexpressible and full of glory ...*" (I Peter 1:8-9) ... 24 carat joy!

Prayer:

God of glory, how I thank You for Your precious Holy Spirit within me and surrounding me, even through the most difficult moments of life! By Your grace, I have been made not just a conqueror, but more than a conqueror – one who not only survives life's trials, but who comes out stronger than I went in. Amen.

20 –
TREASURES OF CONFINEMENT

*"… My circumstances have turned out
for the greater progress of the gospel."*

Philippians 1:12

Paul saw his imprisonment as a God-send. He told the Philippians that it not only enabled the Gospel to break into new audiences, but it also emboldened the churches he led. And there were other blessings too, ones that even he could not have imagined!

He wrote to Timothy from his final prison in Rome saying that *"the word of God is not imprisoned,"* (II,

2:9). He could never have guessed the effect that his words, written two thousand years ago and two thousand kilometres away, would have on the likes of me in our present lockdown!

"... By grace you have been saved through faith; and that not of yourselves, it is the gift of God; not as a result of works, so that no one may boast ..."; "... We are His workmanship, created in Christ Jesus for good works, which God prepared beforehand so that we would walk in them ..."; "... He who began a good work in you will perfect it until the day of Christ Jesus ..."; "... My God will supply all your needs according to His riches in glory in Christ Jesus ..."; "... For you have died and your life is hidden with Christ in God ..."; "... The things which you have heard from me in the presence of many witnesses, entrust these to faithful men who will be able to teach others also." ... and so, so much more!

I am barely even scraping the surface of Paul's prison writings. They have laid the foundation of biblical Christianity, brought untold souls to salvation and inspired churches and civilisations to transform human history. Words that would never have been written, had not Paul been imprisoned.

It may be very small fry by comparison, but if any blessing at all has come to you through the pages of this devotional, know this: it has come to you courtesy of the Corona virus pandemic.

Prayer:

> Dear Lord, help me not to ask 'Why?' in the negative, but in the positive. As Paul himself prayed for his hearers from prison, open the eyes of my heart that I might know "*... what is the hope of [Your] calling, what are the riches of the glory of [Your] inheritance ... and what is the surpassing greatness of [Your] power ...*" (Ephesians 1:18-19) Amen.

21 – MANASSEH

"When he was in distress, he entreated the Lord his God and humbled himself greatly before the God of his fathers. When he prayed to Him, He was moved by his entreaty and heard his supplication, and brought him again to Jerusalem to his kingdom. Then Manasseh knew that the Lord was God."

II Kings 33:12-13

Manasseh! His story is difficult for those who don't understand the Fall of man and the depths to which our race can sink, and who therefore do not appreciate the magnitude of God's grace.

Manasseh was a horrible individual. I once heard evangelist Billy Graham describe him as perhaps the wickedest person who ever lived. He was the son of King Hezekiah, a godly ruler who had once led Judah back to God. But when he succeeded the throne, Manasseh undid all his father's good work and inflicted much more damage beside.

He set up the worship of Baal and Asherah in the Jerusalem temple, put up shrines to pagan gods throughout the land, introduced child sacrifice and even participated in the cult of Moloch by sacrificing his own son.

For decades he persecuted any prophet who dared speak out against him.

"... But God! ..." ... These words were later used by one who described himself as *"chief of sinners"*, the apostle Paul, in reference to a God who transforms instruments of darkness into children of light. God judged Manasseh by sending him into captivity. Manasseh repented, was restored to his throne, cleansed the temple and led Judah back to God.

Many people do not accept the reality of sin, preferring to believe that, in and of ourselves, we are essentially good people. They might rather Manasseh's unsavoury story end with an act of divine retribution. But to a convicted sinner under no illusions of personal merit, without excuse before a holy God, Manasseh is a candle of hope, a treasure of darkness.

Prayer:

Lord Jesus, You said that when the Holy Spirit came, He would *"convict the world concerning sin and righteousness and judgement."* (John 16:8) May I never forget that the only righteousness to satisfy You is that which comes as a gift, provided for sinners by Your precious blood. May the grace that supplied this gift overflow through my life in mercy to all have yet to see. Amen.

22 – AND IT WAS NIGHT

"So when [Jesus] had dipped the morsel, He took and gave it to Judas, the son of Simon Iscariot. After the morsel, Satan then entered into him. Therefore, Jesus said to him, 'What you do, do quickly.' … After receiving the morsel he went out immediately; and it was night."

John 13:26-27, 30

Any doubts of God's power over Satan can be for-ever dispelled from the moment Jesus passed the morsel to Judas. Satan is a fallen angel – the most prominent of his kind, yes, but neither omniscient nor omnipresent, and certainly without power to do anything God has not allowed. So Satan entered Judas to do God's will.

"... And it was night."

The night was not just physical. It was a time of spiritual darkness, but a moment that contained the most glorious act in redemption history, when God would weave Satan's diabolical scheme into His perfect plan for mankind. When God provided His Lamb for the slaughter, His greatest enemies had no understanding of Whom they were now glorifying, otherwise *"they would not have crucified the Lord of glory."* (I Corinthians 2:8)

Earlier in John's Gospel, Jesus had alluded to this moment: *"Night is coming,"* He said, *"when no man can work."* (John 9:4) The night had now come. Man's work had ceased, but in that deep darkness, protected from the natural eye and shielded from human assistance, the Creator was fearfully and wonderfully at work, weaving into one redemptive transaction Christ's death and our birth.

Prayer:

> Lord, I thank You for the wonders that I cannot see and for the certainty that You are at work in the night as in the day. Thank You for Your Holy Spirit, given now to me, enabling me to see, to know and to understand, that in the dark You remain in control. Amen.

23 – A GRAIN OF WHEAT

"Truly, truly, I say to you, unless a grain of wheat falls into the earth and dies, it remains alone; but if it dies, it bears much fruit."

John 12:24

With these words Jesus was preparing His disciples for the Cross, explaining that it is not possible to re-create life without death. His earthly body, dead and buried, was to be understood as a grain of wheat, planted in the soil, helpless until the forces of nature multiplied it after its own kind.

Jesus' death became the seed of His own bodily resurrection; it also became the source of our spiritual life and the sign of our future bodily resurrection. Our life and glorious hope could not exist without the night of His falling. What blindness to doubt the possibility of life after death, when even nature cries out that there cannot be life before it!

And so to us! The cycle of death-then-life is not only something we have benefitted from; it's something we're called to replicate, if we too wish to regenerate. Paul put it this way to the Corinthians, "*So then, death works in us, but life in you.*" (II Corinthians 4:12)? Is this not what Jesus Himself taught His disciples, when He said, "*He who has found his life will lose it, and he who has lost his life for My sake will find it.*" (Matthew 10:39)?

Or James Calvert, the 19th century missionary to South Pacific cannibals, when asked if he and his companions didn't realise how much they were endangering their lives, who replied simply, "*We died before we left!*" Or the early Christian author, Tertullian, who wrote, "*The blood of the martyrs is the seed of the church.*"

Who were all these people? Simply the progeny of Christ's death, disciples who apprehended the wonder of light out of darkness, and who planted their lives in the soil of a better resurrection for themselves and a harvest which is us. How contradictory for Christians to be afraid of the dark, when only by embracing it can we enter life … and be done with fear.

Prayer:

>Lord, if there is fear of the night in me, I ask you to expose it to the light, that I may not run from the darkness, but find Christ and embrace Him right there in it. In that place, be my unshakeable hope, my source of faith for a harvest of souls and my strength of example to any who would follow. Amen.

24 – NIGHT
IS AS DAY

"If I say, 'Surely the darkness will over-
whelm me, and the light around me
will be night,' even the darkness is not
dark to You, and the night is as bright
as the day. Darkness and light are alike
to You."

Psalm 139:11-12

We need to appreciate that darkness is not a problem to God. God is light and needs no external aids
to see and function perfectly. He works equally well
in what we call night or day, uninfluenced by the
cycles that govern our activities.

Sometimes I think God's greatest restriction on

earth is us! Why else would He sometimes make more progress in our darkness than in our daylight? In the darkness, when or best efforts are forced to cease, are we not more likely to depend on Him?

I marvel at the enormous strides God has made among His people during the Corona virus lockdown. The number of people participating in collective prayer in our local church has doubled; we now gather daily instead of weekly; and the quality and intensity of many prayer lives are almost unrecognisable. Walking through the valley of Corona virus, some of us have never been more alive. The church is flourishing and the term 'confinement' is a complete misnomer.

Under this novel form of house arrest, Christians have returned to talking over the fence with their neighbours and are often surprised to find that it is they who bring God into the conversation! Then there's the internet highway. Today, sitting on my living room sofa, I spent an hour teaching the Bible to a passionate team of emerging Christian leaders in an underground house church in a communist state. I have just had to re-schedule my meeting with them next week because it clashes with another meeting in Norway. I normally engage in overseas mission twice a year; under so-called lockdown it seems to have become twice a week!

Yes, Jesus said that when night comes no man can work, but God is not a man. *"He who watches over*

Israel neither slumbers nor sleeps," (Psalm 121:4) and sometimes He delights to bring out His most precious and abundant treasures in what we call night.

Prayer:

> Lord, how I thank You that You are unhindered by the things that so easily overwhelm us; that You are able to accomplish in the night what we cannot in the day! In the hours of night and in the seasons of darkness, Lord, show us Your ways and display Your wonderful works. Amen.

25 – CREATURES OF DAY

"People sleep at night and get drunk at night. But not us! Since we're creatures of Day, let's act like it. Walk out into the daylight sober, dressed up in faith, love, and the hope of salvation ... All of us who look forward to his Coming stay ready, with the glistening purity of Jesus' life as a model for our own."

I Thessalonians 5:7-8;
I John 3:3, The Message

In the Bible, darkness is a metaphor for spiritual slumber and sin, and the human race has been shrouded in both since the Fall of Adam and Eve. In the Old Testament, Isaiah spoke of darkness covering the earth and deep darkness the peoples, and in the New Testament Paul describes the forces of evil at work in the world as *'this present darkness.'*

The spectre of darkness hangs over the world with different intensities, according to the times. In the days leading up to the Crucifixion, the darkness thickened as the glory of Christ shone even brighter.

Similarly, in the days preceding the return of Jesus, God's people will shine with a radiant glow. Paul says we are to be *"blameless and innocent, children of God above reproach in the midst of a crooked and perverse generation, among whom you appear as lights in the world."* (Philippians 2:15)

Christ sees the church as His 'treasure of darkness' ... a people who *"do not participate in the unfruitful deeds of darkness"* but are *"filled with the Spirit, ... cleansed ... by the washing of water with the word ..., having no spot or wrinkle or any such thing; ... holy and blameless."* (Ephesians 5:11, 18, 26-27)

Thus darkness offsets the shining image of a pure people, vigilant and prayerful, awake to the times and seasons, knowing that 'the Moment' will come like a thief in the night, in the twinkling of an eye; a stand-out company who shine ever brighter as the Day draws near.

Prayer:

My God, to think that I am Your treasure of darkness, Your bounty from a sin-spoiled creation! To think that we, the church, are the priceless purchase of Christ's precious blood! Shine brightly through us today, that the world around us might see Him whose we are and whose likeness we bear, and whose reward we will be on the day of His Coming. Amen.

26 – YOU ARE LIGHT

"… You were formerly darkness, but now you are Light in the Lord; walk as children of Light."

Ephesians 5:8

When we see the promise of 'treasures of darkness', we tend to think of our blessing. But what about God? What are *His* treasures? What an incredible thought that we have been drawn out of deep darkness to be the pleasure of His eyes! The God who said, *"Let there be light!"* at the dawn of creation, is the same God who spoke into the spiritual darkness of fallen man and created a people of light, which is us, His church.

The same Jesus who said, *"I am the Light of the world!"* (John 8:12) also said, *"You are the light of the world!"* (Matthew 5:14) The light which we now are is not of our making, but of His. We are not the product of religious effort, but the fruit of His creative word, the Gospel. Listen to Paul earlier in Ephesians: *"... Even when we were dead in our trans-gressions, [God] made us alive together with Christ ..."* (Ephesians 2:5) We are the light that God created out of darkness! His treasure! Created by God, for God.

So, what of us then? How should we respond to this incredible identity? Shine! Just shine for Him! If we are children of Light, there can only be one re-sponse: walk as children of Light! As Paul had just written to the same Ephesians, *"... Put on the new self, which in the likeness of God has been created in righteousness and holiness of the truth."* (Ephesians 4:24)

We are the work of His creation! This realisation of what we have been made to be, by God's grace, not our effort, is the inspiration we need in order to live it out. Wow! I have been created, wholly and exclu-sively by an act of God, with God's personal DNA of righteousness and holiness of the truth woven into the very fabric of my being!

How do I thank Him? Just live it. Just walk it. Get out into the world and glow for your Creator as His treasure of darkness!

Prayer:

Oh Lord, what an incredible thing You have done! Just as the natural creation in Adam, so is the new creation in Christ! As the Psalmist wrote, *"... I am fearfully and wonderfully made!"* (Psalm 139:14). By Your grace and in the power of Your Holy Spirit, enable me to shine as Your light in the world as one who brings great pleasure to Your eyes! Amen.

27 – ZEL

"It started when God said, 'Light up the darkness!' and our lives filled up with light as we saw and understood God in the face of Christ, all bright and beautiful."

II Corinthians 4:6, The Message

The Scriptures are clear that Christ will one day return in glory, but before then His light will shine brightly through those who have already seen His face. Thirty-four days into the dark spectre of the current lockdown, this was the diary entry of church secretary, Zel:

"What am I going to remember about 2020? Not the darkness of the coronavirus pandemic or global lockdown. I will be remembering that this

was when I was completely, '360' changed ... a completely new woman, completely surrendered to God! I am 33 and have been a Christian for many years, but I have never, in all that time, experienced anything like this. I am completely transformed. I see with new eyes. It's completely different.

"For the first time in my Christian life, I can truly say that I am building a relationship with Jesus. I really do love Him. I am bound to Him. I am His, to do whatever His will commands. I ask the Lord every day to please use me as He sees fit. I ask the Holy Spirit to be in my heart, in my thoughts, in my mind, in my eyes, in my ears, in my mouth, in my hands, in my feet ... just to take over!

"This is just amazing. The words I'm hearing from others are showing me that this is not just me. And the fact that God Almighty is using me, putting things on my heart, that He thinks I'm worth speaking through ...! ... But I'm not speaking – it's not me, it's Him!

"He's so good, so gracious, so patient, so kind ... He's awesome! God has got a big plan. Something big is going to happen. People are going to get rooted and standing firm. When this pandemic is over, we are going to be rising, stronger than ever. There is definitely a move of God going on!"

Prayer:

Hallelujah! Thank You, God, that You cause the brightest lights to shine out of the darkest nights. Show me the face of Christ today! Lay hold of my life now, that I might lay hold of You. Shine on me, Lord, and cause me to shine brighter for You than ever before. Amen.

28 – SAMUEL

"Now the boy Samuel was ministering to the Lord before Eli. And word from the Lord was rare in those days, visions were infrequent."

I Samuel 3:1

Light is a metaphor for the word of God. *"Your word is a lamp to my feet and a light to my path ... The entrance of Your words gives light,"* the Psalms declare. (119:105, 130) And so, there is no greater mark of spiritual darkness than the absence of God's word.

Samuel's life spans the rise of Israel from one of its deepest spiritual troughs – a period defined by the absence of revelation from the Lord – to the triumphant days of David's kingdom, a period still looked back upon today as the halcyon age of Israel's ancient history.

To herald this spectacular lift, God revealed His word to His messenger, Samuel. Whereas I Samuel chapter 3 begins with, *"the word of God was rare,"* it ends with, *"... the Lord revealed Himself to Samuel ... by the word of the Lord,"* and then chapter 4 begins with, *"... the word of Samuel came to all Israel."*

The journey of a people from darkness to light was, as it always has been, lit up by the spread of the word of God, the same word that in the beginning spoke light into being, and later became flesh in Christ Himself ... *"... the true Light which, coming into the world, enlightens every man."* (John 1:9)

This rise of Israel to its most glorious day began on a dark night in a desecrated temple, where the sinfulness of Eli's sons had all but caused the lamp of God to go out in Israel. In that place the word of God came to a boy, then through a boy to a nation, and then, from the splendour of David's Kingdom, to the surrounding peoples.

Darkness still abounds. *"The god of this world has blinded the minds of the unbelieving so that they might not see the light of the gospel of the glory of Christ ..."* (II Corinthians 4:4) But every so often, a child discovers the most priceless treasure of the night, the voice of God. The boy becomes a messenger, the Gospel is declared, and the world is changed.

Prayer:

Dear Lord, thank You for Your promise that *"the earth will be filled with the knowledge of the glory of the Lord, as the waters cover the sea."* (Habakkuk 2:14) And thank You that all it takes is for a child to hear Your voice in the night. Lord, up and down this land and all across the nations, waken up a new generation of Samuels. Lord, speak to me also, I pray. Amen.

29 – LIGHT INTO DARKNESS

"From the very first day, we were there, taking it all in – we heard it with our own ears, saw it with our own eyes, verified it with our own hands. The Word of Life appeared right before our eyes; we saw it happen! And now we're telling you in most sober prose that what we witnessed was, incredibly, this: The infinite Life of God himself took shape before us … This, in essence, is the message we heard from Christ and are passing on to you: God is light, pure light; there's not a trace of darkness in him."

I John 1:1-2, 5, The Message

We have seen how treasure is concealed in dark paces and how it can emerge from dark places, but John, like few others, shows us how to bring treasure into dark places. John wrote his Gospel, three epistles and Revelation as an old man. He probably produced these works as late as the AD80s or even 90s, a period of heavily intensifying persecution.

In Foxe's Book of Martyrs, we are told that John was the only one of the Twelve not to die a martyr's death, but only by being miraculously delivered from an attempt to boil him in a cauldron of oil! Tradition has it that before he died in Ephesus, he was banished to the Island of Patmos, where he penned his apocalyptic revelation of end-time events.

John may have been in his early teens when first called by Jesus. Now, perhaps 60 years later, most of his early peers are long gone. But with a spark that has never left his eye, he gazes back through many years of trial, and draws upon days of encounter that shine as brightly now as they did when they first overwhelmed His life.

I can imagine the ageing John becoming a boy again as he still stares spellbound at the feeding of 5,000 with just five loaves and two fish, as he visualises the bound corpse of Lazarus walking out of his tomb after four days dead, as he reclines once more on Jesus' breast, and testifies with pristine clarity to *"what appeared right before our eyes."*

John never lost the unquenchable glow of past encounter. Right to the very end, he allowed its pure light to extinguish the present darkness also. Seasons of trial are the time to remember and to testify to things once done that can never be undone, things once known that can never be unknown, to bring their Light into the present, and for their glow to light up our life once more.

Prayer:

> God of Light, thank You that what You did once can never cease to shine. Thank You that the Light which once entered this world, and once lit up my life, will never be overpowered. Remind me to 'polish' these treasures daily in my mind, that their sparkle might never leave my eye or their glow leave my life, for as long as I live! Amen.

30 – LIGHT TO THE GENTILES

"Paul and Barnabas spoke out boldly and said, 'It was necessary that the word of God be spoken to you first; since you repudiate it and judge yourselves unworthy of eternal life, behold, we are turning to the Gentiles. For so the Lord has commanded us, "I have placed You as a light for the Gentiles, that You may bring salvation to the end of the earth."'"

Acts 13:46–47

Jesus' rejection by His own people was the saddest moment of their history, the anticipation of which moved Jesus to weep over Jerusalem. But by delivering Jesus over to a Roman cross, the chief priests were actually exporting the Gospel to the Gentiles, ignorantly preparing the way for the global mission to which Abram was originally called.

Many forget that Christianity is Jewish in origin. Jesus was born, circumcised and raised a Jew. He quoted Moses and the Jewish prophets in His teaching. His first apostles were all Jews. The first churches worshipped in the temple, and also in the synagogues of Israel and around the Mediterranean world. Apart from Luke, every New Testament author was Jewish. And the same New Testament makes it very clear that God is far from finished with the Jews yet.

But the greatest error of Jewish history – the rejection of their Messiah – was, as ever, woven into the perfect plan of an all-knowing God. The God who causes light to shine out of darkness is the God who would drown out Jerusalem's cries of "Crucify Him!", by a Gospel message that in coming millennia would shape the nations of the world. As Paul explained to the Romans, *"... by their transgression salvation has come to the Gentiles."* (Romans 11:11)

Out of Jewish darkness came light to the Gentiles! One true Jew, the aged Simeon, had declared over the infant Jesus in the temple, *"Now Lord, You are releasing Your bond-servant to depart in peace, ... for my eyes have seen Your salvation, ... a Light of revelation to the Gentiles, and the glory of Your people Israel."* (Luke 2:29-30, 32)

Christ's glory was to be revealed only through the rejection of the Cross; and the darkness in which His own spurned Him, birthed the light by which those afar off now see.

Prayer:

> Father in Heaven, How I thank You for sending Christ to be a Light of revelation to us who were so far off. Thank You that the rejection of His own created my opportunity to receive; that one people's temporary darkness became the eternal Light of every nation on earth. Lord, I pray that any who have rejected You will see Your light in us, Your people, today. In Jesus' name I ask, Amen.

31 – REDEMPTIVE ANALOGY

"… Men of Athens, I observe that you are very religious in all respects. For while I was passing through and examining the objects of your worship, I also found an altar with this inscription, 'TO AN UNKNOWN GOD.' Therefore, what you worship in ignorance, this I proclaim to you."

Acts 17:22–23

Earlier on in the chapter, we read of how provoked Paul was by a city full of idols. And now, it appears they worshipped so many gods that they even had an altar for one they had yet to discover! It was in this expression of unusual darkness that Paul saw a chink of light, a doorway of opportunity for the Gospel.

In his wonderful book, *Eternity in Their Hearts*, Don Richardson writes of redemptive analogies to be discovered in every unreached culture – customs and beliefs hidden in their own folklore, sovereignly deposited by a God whose earthly messengers are yet to arrive. Richardson calls this phenomenon 'the Melchidedek factor', referring to a mysterious king who was somehow connected with God at the same time as, and yet apart from, Abram.

Richardson cites example after example of tribes whose own seers and traditions kept them waiting for the day their great hope would appear. While we understand that the Gospel of Christ alone reveals the way of salvation, how inspiring it is to know that God's reach is so much greater than the extent of our travels!

How wonderful that God is able to use absolutely anything He has created to lead the most unreached people to the light of Christ's Gospel! How amazing that such a God would even step into the spiritual darkness of eastern astrologers and use the stars they worshipped to guide them to the infant Messiah – at the very time when the ruler of God's chosen people was trying to put that Child of Promise to death!

So much higher are His thoughts than our thoughts,

and His ways than our ways, that He will use the deepest darkness to prepare the way for the most glorious light!

Prayer:

> Almighty God, may I never limit You to the extent of human reach. Help me to understand that Your sovereignty over the entire cosmos is so much greater than the tiny spheres that we, Your people, have yet to see beyond. By Your Spirit, give us Your eyes to discover, and Your boldness to walk through, the doorways of light we so easily miss without You. Amen.

32 – EPHESUS

*"And many of those who practised
magic brought their books together
and began burning them in the sight
of everyone; and they counted up
the price of them and found it fifty
thousand pieces of silver. So the word
of the Lord was growing mightily and
prevailing."*

Acts 19:19–20

After Rome and Alexandria, Ephesus was the largest city of the Roman Empire of its day, a bustling metropolis that drew travellers, traders and mystics from everywhere between the Far East, Egypt and Rome itself, and with a strong Jewish presence there too. Around 250,000 people lived within the city walls alone.

Ephesus was renowned as a centre for magical practices and for the worship of around fifty gods, but people and deities alike all lived under the shadow of the Temple of Artemis, just outside the city walls, one of the Seven Wonders of the Ancient World. Twice a week, a procession would march from the temple around the city, just in case anyone needed reminding of the dominance of Artemis the Great.

Cue the Apostle Paul!

This dominion of darkness was the place chosen by God for Paul to settle and teach for two whole years, longer than anywhere else on his missionary journeys. The result? Everyone in western Turkey heard the Gospel of Christ, with the word of God *"growing mightily and prevailing,"* and even the demons talking about Jesus and Paul.

When converts fuelled an enormous bonfire with books of magic arts valued at 50,000 days' wages and the god-smiths of Artemis feared for their livelihoods, Paul was forced to leave, but not before establishing a vibrant church to whom he would later write a glorious epistle, laying an astonishing theological foundation upon which Christ still builds His church today!

To quote another great missionary, C. T. Studd, *"Some want to live within the sound of church or chapel bell; I want to run a rescue shop, within a yard of hell."*

Ephesus. Treasure of darkness.

Prayer:

> God of Wonders, thank You that this world has no god too great for You to topple in a moment. By the power of Your Holy Spirit and the unstoppable truth of Your word, take us, Your church, to the seats of darkness in this world - not to find another stall in the market place, but to herald the arrival of a God too great to do anything other than take over the hearts of men and women. Amen.

33 – THE CROWN OF RIGHTEOUSNESS

"… Momentary, light affliction is producing for us an eternal weight of glory far beyond all comparison."

II Corinthians 4:17

What do you think Paul meant by 'momentary light afflictions?'

In the same epistle, he describes the suffering he has experienced and it is a gruelling list. *"In far more labours, in far more imprisonments, beaten times without number, often in danger of death. Five times I received from the Jews thirty-nine lashes. Three times*

I was beaten with rods, once I was stoned, three times I was shipwrecked, a night and a day I have spent in the deep. I have been on frequent journeys, in dangers from rivers, dangers from robbers, dangers from my countrymen, dangers from the Gentiles, dangers in the city, dangers in the wilderness, dangers on the sea, dangers among false brethren; I have been in labour and hardship, through many sleepless nights, in hunger and thirst, often without food, in cold and exposure. Apart from such external things, there is the daily pressure on me of concern for all the churches." (II Corinthians 11:23–28)

One wonders whether Paul's experiences should ever be considered light! But when writing to the Philippians he also used the phrase, *"the fellowship of Christ's sufferings,"* (Philippians 3:10). It is clear that at times he experienced a deep communion with Jesus and identified with our Lord's suffering on the cross. There were times when the prospect of his own death even became attractive to him.

I once visited the Mamertine Prison in Rome, where some think Paul penned his last letter to Timothy. He wrote: *"I am already being poured out as a drink offering, and the time of my departure has come. I have fought the good fight, I have finished the course, I have kept the faith; in the future there is laid up for me the crown of righteousness, which the Lord, the righteous Judge, will award to me on that day; and not only to me, but also to all who have loved His appearing."* (II Timothy 4:6-8)

Suffering for Christ is a blessing that few of us actively seek, yet it offers a two-fold treasure: closeness to Christ in this life and a crown of righteousness in the life to come.

Prayer:

> My Father, Jesus told us that we are blessed when people insult and persecute us because of Him. In such moments, may I find myself drawn closer to Him, and filled with joy in the assurance of Your eternal reward. (Matthew 5:11–12) Amen.

34 – RICKY
AND JULIE

"… That you may proclaim the excellencies of Him who has called you out of darkness into His marvellous light."

I Peter 2:9

Julie had her first child at the age of fifteen and her second child at seventeen. By the time she reached eighteen she was a heroin addict. Her life spiralled out of control and her children were taken into foster care. She entered a long dark night until, at the age of twenty-five, she cried out to God and found Jesus Christ in a Teen Challenge rehabilitation centre.

Ricky, another deeply insecure teenager, took to alcohol and drugs and his life became more chaotic than he could ever have imagined. At the age of twenty-seven he hit the buffers. Then, like Julie, he found Jesus in a Teen Challenge centre. In his early Christian years he struggled before he finally surrendered his life to God.

Ricky and Julie, now born again believers, met in 2011 and were married in 2013. Later that year they launched an outreach from Glasgow City Church Café called Street Connect. Seven years later they lead a team of 20 paid staff and over 70 volunteers in the Central Belt of Scotland. They bring life and hope to some of the most desperate people on our streets.

Julie's two children were wonderfully restored to her and have now entered adulthood knowing what it is to live in a stable, loving, Christian home. She and Ricky also have two young children now growing up in the love of Jesus. Julie says, "My life has been unrecognisably transformed," and Ricky describes himself as "blessed beyond my wildest dreams!" Their family is a trophy of grace and their ministry is undeniable evidence of the life-giving power of the Gospel of Jesus Christ.

Their testimony is one of faith, love and excellence in all they do, as they *"proclaim the excellencies of Him who has called [them] out of darkness into His marvellous light."*

Ricky and Julie are treasures of darkness. There are many more to be discovered.

Prayer:

Lord, how I thank You for the power of Your Spirit and Your word to enter the darkest chaos and transform lives. Thank you that among the most hopeless of souls are tomorrow's trophies of grace and leaders of change! Show me today the part I can play in taking Your Gospel to a world of desperate need. In Jesus' name, use me, I ask. Amen.

35 – LAST DAYS

*"… Creation itself also will be set free
from its slavery to corruption into the
freedom of the glory of the children
of God. For we know that the whole
creation groans and suffers the pains of
childbirth together until now."*

Romans 8:21-22

As I approached writing the last few days of *Treasures of Darkness*, my thoughts turned towards the greatest display of God's glory that creation will ever witness. True to the theme of these devotionals, it will emerge from the deepest shades of darkness.

I did not set out to write this series with the Last Days in mind, but along the way it has become clear that they are its proper conclusion.

At the start of the current global pandemic, I became quickly convinced that Christians must focus on what lies beyond it and prepare themselves spiritually. Jesus called his followers 'the light of the world.' We need as never before to be lighthouses of hope and certainty in the darkness which the Bible warns is coming.

Romans chapter 8 talks of the pains of childbirth, so let me be honest about my experience. There were times when I was younger that I gave thanks for not being a woman! Five times I have sat in relative comfort (and certainly without pain), watching in awe as my wife heroically delivered four sons and a daughter, some of them weighing nearly 10 lbs! In consequence I hold every mother in the highest honour and respect.

Only a mother can understand the fullness of joy that follows the birth of a beautiful new creation, the gift of God. Only a mother can appreciate the connection between herself and her own child who has made the journey from the darkness of the womb into a world of light and life.

Beyond this age of human history, the Bible tells of a new heaven and a new earth. But before then, the pain of labour. That glorious future is a story of light out of darkness, life out of death, salvation from suffering, and joy flowing out of pain. The church's future is one of affliction and of deliverance, of anguish and of bliss, of darkness and of treasure.

To fail to see these things is to be unprepared for the Last Days!

Prayer:

> Lord Jesus, as I turn my thoughts to Your second coming, I know that You have already walked the path that lies ahead for us. Thank You that Your tomb became the womb out of which Your resurrected body rose. May that same hope be my guiding light, and in times of darkness help me to shine as a child of the Day that is to come. Amen.

36 – TREASURES OF PATMOS

"I, John, your brother and fellow partaker in the tribulation and kingdom and perseverance which are in Jesus, was on the island called Patmos because of the word of God and the testimony of Jesus ... I was in the Spirit; and behold, a throne was standing in heaven, and One sitting on the throne. And He who was sitting was like a jasper stone and a sardius in appearance; and there was a rainbow around the throne, like an emerald in appearance."

Revelation 1:9; 4:2–3

With the End Times foremost in my mind, I return to John, 'the beloved disciple.' Tradition has it that when he was an old man the Emperor Domitian banished him to the island of Patmos for preaching the gospel. Domitian was a paranoid tyrant and a dangerous enemy but the exile he imposed could no more silence John than imprisonment by Nero had silenced Paul.

From Patmos John described glorious visions of Christ and heaven, embellished with gemstones of iron-tinted jasper, blood-red sardius, and a rainbow that was somehow emerald-like in appearance.

The Book of Revelation is the climax of the Scriptures and the text literally confers a blessing on all who read it (- a promise made by none of the other sixty-five books!). So why, then, have I been reading it less than any other book in the New Testament, until the present lockdown? Could it be that, like many others, the comforts of modern life have steered me away from its apocalyptic narrative? And yet this book literally brims over with the Bible's crown jewels.

Dr Richard Bauckham describes Revelation as a gathering together and raising to new heights of Bible prophecy; a final, literal fulfilment of the Lord's Prayer: "*Thy Kingdom come, Thy will be done on earth as it is in heaven.*"

This is the book of *"things which must take place after these things,"* (1:19) an awesome vision of hope written to inspire an unstoppable people through very difficult days.

Prayer:

> Dear Lord, thank You that when we hit the darkest days, we discover in Your word the most beautiful treasures. Bless my eyes that I might see, and my ears that I might hear today. May Your word enable me to see this world as it truly is, and to discover the things that are to come as I have not seen them before. In Jesus' name, I pray. Amen.

37 – THE LAMB TRIUMPHANT

"... Worthy is the Lamb that was slain to receive power and riches and wisdom and might and honour and glory and blessing."

Revelation 5:12

Nowhere does the Bible teach that following Christ is an escape from suffering. Rather, Jesus said that discipleship would be the *cause* of suffering. Had He not warned his followers, *"... If they persecuted Me, they will also persecute you"*? (John 15:20)

A major symbol of Christ in Revelation is the Lamb. John's Gospel had introduced Jesus as *"the Lamb of God who takes away the sin of the world."* (John 1:29)

As such, He was not just our substitute but our example. His disciples must be willing to follow His sacrificial path to glory.

Hence, the great reward for those who "*... overcame [Satan] because of the blood of the Lamb and because of the word of their testimony, and **they did not love their life even when faced with death**.*" (Revelation 12:11, emphasis mine)

Revelation was written for a church under intense persecution. It fortified believers by fixing their eyes on the Lamb triumphant, Jesus Christ, who conquered death and now held the keys of death and Hades.

By exalting Christ as Lamb, worshippers declare the cross to be a place of triumph, not of defeat. They are also comforted in the loss of loved ones who have paid the ultimate price, and encouraged to overcome such a test should they ever face it themselves. Those who share His suffering will also share His glory.

The book culminates in a new heaven and a new earth. What a journey the old apostle has taken us on, from gazing into heaven in chapter 4 to witnessing the new Jerusalem descending from above in chapter 21! And what a message of courage and hope: God is in charge, not Satan or any wicked earthly power!

Prayer:

Almighty God, how I thank You that You not only offer the certain hope of a glorious future, but also the confidence that, no matter what suffering Your people may have to endure, You are in control. Fill me with Your grace and peace, that I may stay close to You, remaining sober and alert, ever focused on the Lamb now exalted. In Jesus' name, I pray. Amen.

38 – THE GOD OF EVERYTHING

*"Then I saw a new heaven and a new
earth; for the first heaven and the
first earth passed away, and there is
no longer any sea. And I saw the holy
city, new Jerusalem, coming down out
of heaven from God, made ready as a
bride adorned for her husband."*

Revelation 21:1

The God of redemption is also the Lord of the cosmos.

Sin not only infected Adam like a virus, but it corrupted everything mankind touched, including our relationships with each other and even the planet we were appointed to steward.

But – hallelujah! – in Jesus, God provided a lasting remedy which dealt with the sin virus at source.

The blood of the Lamb who was slain was the once-and-for-all solution to the root problem of sin. And the outflow of Jesus Christ's redeeming power extends to absolutely everything that has in any way, directly or indirectly, been affected by sin. One day, He will return to rule in righteousness that which He has redeemed.

The Book of Revelation contains the wonderful message that in the Last Days the church of Jesus Christ does not merely survive the tribulation. It gathers in an end-time harvest drawn from all of Adam's descendants ... "... *a great multitude which no one could count, from every nation and all tribes and peoples and tongues.*" (Revelation 7:9)

There will be a great trumpet blast and a loud cry will go up from Heaven: "*The kingdom of the world has become the kingdom of our Lord and of His Christ; and He will reign forever and ever.*" (Revelation 11:15) It will not be a kingdom located in some remote galaxy, but one that occupies a redeemed Planet Earth.

In the final chapter of the Bible, we return to the Garden of Eden, a garden that now finds itself located in a magnificent, bejewelled city of which the writer says, "*The nations will walk by its light, and the kings of the earth will bring their glory into it."* (Revelation 21:24)

Prayer:

> God of everything, how I thank You that You will not walk away from this planet in defeat. How awesome is the purchasing power of Your blood! How wonderful that You will one day return to rule all creation in righteousness! Lord Jesus, in the coming days help me never to lose sight of the glory that is to be revealed. Amen.

39 – TREASURE FROM CARNAGE

"And we know that in all things God works for the good of those who love Him, who have been called according to His purpose."

Romans 8:28, NIV

Today's entry is by my dearest friend, John Gibson. I am deeply moved and more grateful than I can express that, seven months after his and Isobel's devastating loss of their son, he has agreed to share a treasure of greater personal cost than most of us could begin to imagine:

"It was Sunday, 7.45am when the door-bell rang. Two police officers told me that Cameron was dead.

Our wonderful, talented, handsome 24-year old veterinary surgeon son had killed himself earlier that morning, injecting himself with the same drug he had used on many occasions to put animals to sleep. How could our caring, loving, smiling son with a huge circle of friends and a close-knit family have done this? What had gone wrong? What had we done wrong? It was a tragic mystery with no note of explanation left.

"And so, with the carnage and mystery of suicide enveloping us, we threw ourselves into the promises and mysteries of Christ Jesus. We found that God showed us His gentleness and kindness, speaking tenderly and lovingly to us when we were completely broken and could hardly even pray. He offered us a gift of faith to believe that in ALL things – yes, even the heart-breaking death of a son by suicide – He would work for our good. Jesus who held Cameron in His arms in his moment of despair, as the whole of Heaven cried 'No, Cameron, it doesn't have to be this way', respected Cameron's decision, chose not to intervene, and then carried him in the same loving arms into Heaven. Those same nail-scarred arms of Jesus have held us close and carried us in these darkest of days. Faith is a gift; ask Father for His gift of faith for you today and let those loving arms enfold you."

Prayer:

My Father, I thank You for living testimony that there is no place so dark, no carnage so great that Your gentleness and kindness, Your tenderness and love, cannot be found. Thank You that, even at moments when I can barely pray, Your presence is still there and Your arms are so faithful to carry me through. Speak into my heart today. I ask You now for Your gift of faith, to believe that in ALL things You will work for my good. In Jesus' name I ask. Amen.

40 – REFINED SILVER

"The words of the Lord are pure words; as silver tried in a furnace of the earth, refined seven times."

Psalm 12:6

40 Days: Treasures of Darkness is built on the biblical premise that Heaven's brightest enters through Earth's darkest. This is not a mystical idea but a spiritual law, tested and proven in the lives of real people. That is why this devotional has been laced with personal testimonies: those of Janice, myself, Zel, Ricky and Julie. And of course John Gibson's powerful and moving testimony yesterday.

As the end of this series approached, I prayed, *"Lord,*

I believe the truth of 'treasures of darkness' is beyond doubt, capable of withstanding the toughest assaults of life." I dared to challenge God: *"Show me the darkest possible circumstance within my reach and let me put these words to the test."* (That is always a dangerous thing to do with God!)

Almost immediately, my friend John came to my mind and I wished I hadn't made such a challenge. John and Isobel, as you now know, recently lost their beloved son to suicide and, seven months later, are still working through the fall-out.

Somehow I found the courage to call him, but it was not to offer my help. What could I possibly say? Instead I asked for his help and trembled as I did so. *"John,"* I said, *"in this darkness, have you discovered any light?"* When he spoke of God's kindness, I wept. The light John had discovered spilled over to me, as I hope it did to you yesterday morning.

I do not know what lies ahead for dear John and Isobel or indeed for any of us. But I see clearly the pattern of God at work and I hear it resound in the words of the apostle Paul. He described how God plans for us to comfort others:

> *"Blessed be the God and Father of our Lord Jesus Christ, the Father of mercies and God of all comfort, who comforts us in all our affliction so that we will be able to comfort those who are in any affliction with the comfort with which we ourselves are comforted by God. For just as the suffer-*

ings of Christ are ours in abundance, so also our comfort is abundant through Christ. But if we are afflicted, it is for your comfort and salvation; or if we are comforted, it is for your comfort, which is effective in the patient enduring of the same sufferings which we also suffer; and our hope for you is firmly grounded, knowing that as you are sharers of our sufferings, so also you are sharers of our comfort." (II Corinthians 1:3-7)

Prayer:

My Father, as I stand between the afflictions of Earth and the glories of Heaven, I ask You to demonstrate in and through me powers of the age that is to come. I ask for Your grace to shine as Your light in a dark world. Fill me afresh with Your Holy Spirit. Empower me to speak of Jesus Christ and to lead others to the treasures found only in You. Amen.

EPILOGUE

Three months after the 2020 pandemic thrust a bewildered and frightened UK into lockdown, the government's restrictions are now, finally, easing by the week.

Both church and world are beginning to emerge from their bunkers, some bold enough to predict with quiet confidence what the 'new normal' might look like.

Many of us are confident that things to come have already begun. While some have floundered through an unprecedented season in recent history, others have apparently flourished.

As a friend so eloquently put it one of many recent Zoom meetings, the same storm that drives most birds to the shelter of the trees causes eagles to spread their wings, face the storm, harness the elements and soar to heights hitherto unknown.

I am grateful to God that the latter has been by far the greater experience of those around me.

The collective prayer life of my church has flourished beyond recognition. New gifts, abilities and callings have emerged in the lives of next generation leaders.

The shock of the pandemic has been a spiritual defibrillator to the spiritual lives of wanderers and backsliders. Within the fold it has been for some a period of spiritual rest and renewal, for others a time of repentance and reset.

Pastoral care networks have been jolted into action. The inter-church unity movement of which I am a part has intensified and increased in its collaboration.

In my home church, as the world protests racism I daily taste heaven in a congregation of around 30 nationalities, experiencing a oneness and harmony that I have not experienced in 39 years of Christian life.

These are just some of the treasures that gleam brighter than ever in what many would consider one of the darkest moments in living memory

Having based this devotional on the words of the prophet Isaiah, I can think of no one better to conclude …

> *"Arise, shine; for your light has come, and the glory of the Lord has risen upon you. For behold, darkness will cover the earth and deep darkness the peoples; but the Lord will rise upon you and His*

glory will appear upon you. Nations will come to your light, and kings to the brightness of your rising." (Isaiah 60:1-3)

ABOUT THE AUTHOR

Alistair J Matheson

Alistair Matheson is lead pastor of Glasgow City Church and a member of the National Leadership Team of the Apostolic Church UK. Since the 1980s Alistair has been involved in church planting and mission in Scotland, as well as  overseas. Married to Barbara, Alistair has five grown-up children.

UNTITLED

Printed in Great Britain
by Amazon